RAIN FOREST
PEOPLE

Text and Photography by Edward Parker

RAINTREE
STECK-VAUGHN
RSVP PUBLISHERS

A Harcourt Company

Austin   New York
www.raintreesteckvaughn.com

Published by Raintree Steck-Vaughn Publishers, an imprint of Steck-Vaughn Company

Library of Congress Cataloging-in-Publication data is available upon request.

ISBN 0-7398-5242-6

Printed in Hong Kong. Bound in the United States.

1 2 3 4 5 6 7 8 9 0 LB 07 06 05 04 03

Editor: Sarah Doughty
Design: Bernard Higton
Text consultant: Dr. Paul Toyne

Picture acknowledgments:

All photographs are by Edward Parker with the exception of the following: B & C Alexander 7; Still Pictures 4 bottom, 8 (Herbert Giradet), 19 (Mark Edwards), 24 (Nigel Dickinson). Artwork is by Peter Bull.

CONTENTS

① WELCOME TO THE RAIN FOREST

The Inhabited Rain Forest

Some people imagine that the world's rain forests are wild, uninhabited places. In fact, people have lived in rain forests for about a million years. Today, rain forests are home to over 150 million people, who live in settlements ranging from traditional villages to huge cities. Many of these inhabitants are indigenous. This means that they are descended from the people who first lived in the forest. Indigenous people usually live together in small tribal groups and try to carry on their traditional way of life, which involves growing crops and hunting animals. But rain forests are home to a much broader variety of people than just the indigenous population. Many who live in the rain forests today are migrants, who have come from poor areas in search of land on which to grow crops or keep animals. Many come looking for jobs in industries such as mining, logging, or cattle ranching. Most come from the overcrowded towns and cities that have developed in the rain forests during the 20th century.

◀ This man's family has lived in the Amazon rain forest for more than 100 years. His relatives first moved to the area to collect rubber from the trees.

▼ The Amazon rain forest is home to many indigenous people such as this Kayapo Indian boy.

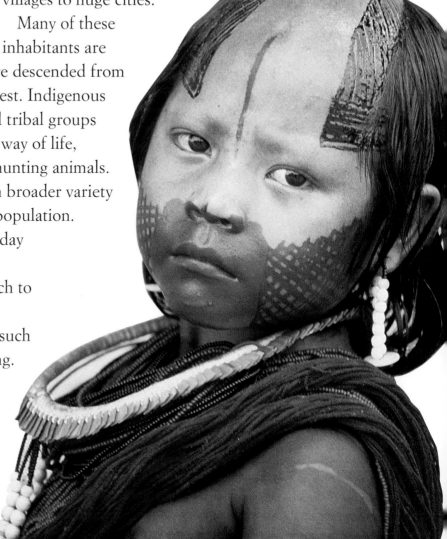

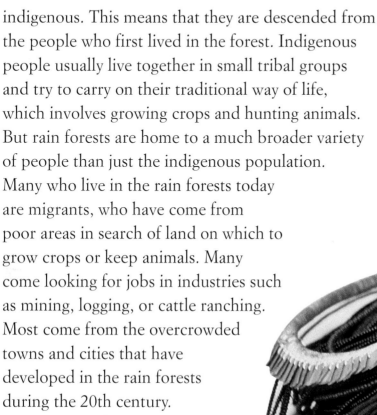

Where Are the Tropical Rain Forests?

The world's tropical rain forests lie along a belt near the Equator, between the tropics of Cancer and Capricorn. The temperatures here are consistently high throughout the year and rainfall is greater than 80 inches (2,000 mm).

The largest area of continuous rain forest on earth is found in the Amazon region of South America. This area is similar in size to the United States, excluding Alaska. Tropical rain forests are also found in parts of Africa, Southeast Asia, the South Pacific, and Australia. This book will look mainly at the people who live in the Amazon rain forest.

◀ Local women walk along the edge of the Udzungwa Mountain forest in Tanzania, East Africa. This forest is protected against deforestation.

▼ A map showing the extent of the world's tropical rain forests today, compared with 500 years ago, before large-scale deforestation began.

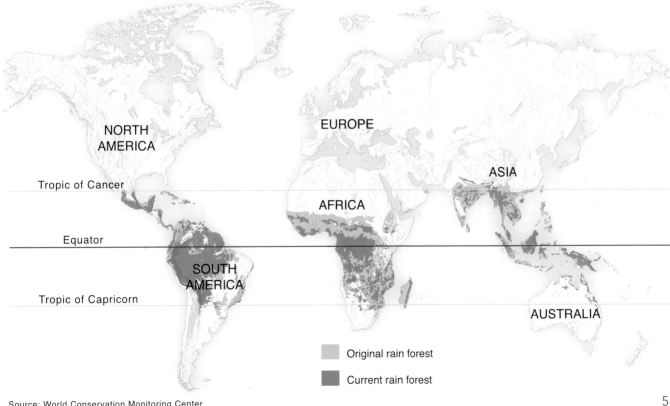

NORTH AMERICA

EUROPE

ASIA

Tropic of Cancer

AFRICA

Equator

SOUTH AMERICA

Tropic of Capricorn

AUSTRALIA

Original rain forest

Current rain forest

Source: World Conservation Monitoring Center

Types of Rain Forest

Scientists today recognize about forty different types of rain forest, but generally divide them into two main categories according to their height above sea level. These are lowland forest and montane forest. Groups of people living there have developed different lifestyles, which suit the type of rain forest they inhabit.

Lowland Rain Forests

Lowland forests are the most widespread rain forests in the world. They also contain the richest communities of trees and plants. Most indigenous peoples, such as the Kayapo and Yanomami Indians of the Amazon, and the Baka pygmies of Cameroon, live in lowland forests. They have survived for thousands of years by carefully managing the rain forest resources. However, the valuable trees in the forest attract loggers who cut down large areas of land.

▲ A Woarani Indian in a dugout canoe in the rain forest of Ecuador in South America.

▼ An indigenous woman from a montane forest near Pasto, in Colombia, South America.

RAIN FOREST SECRETS

THE YALI OF IRIAN JAYA

There are about 20,000 Yali inhabiting the central highlands of the island of Irian Jaya in Indonesia. The Yali live on ridge tops surrounded by cool montane forest, where they cultivate hardy vegetables such as taros, yams, and sweet potatoes in small gardens. They also raise pigs and chickens.

The Yali are expert hunters and use poison-tipped arrows to kill their prey, including small marsupials, such as the tree kangaroo, and the cassowary bird, which is the size of a small ostrich. This Yali elder from the Seng valley in Irian Jaya is a successful hunter. The curved bones he wears around his head are the tusks of wild boar—a symbol of his bravery. The shells around his neck are for decoration and can also be used as currency.

Fascinating Fact

The Baka pygmies of Cameroon collect honey by climbing over 150 feet (50 m) up giant lowland rain forest trees.

Montane Rain Forests

Montane forests can be found on hills and mountains above 3,000 feet (900 m) in tropical areas, where it is generally cooler and damper than in the lowland forests. These forests are often hidden in dense mists, which has given rise to their alternative name, "cloud forests."

Fewer indigenous groups live here. Peoples such as the Awa in Colombia and the Yali in Irian Jaya (Indonesia) have adapted to living in the isolated montane forest. The lack of large navigable rivers, the cool climate, and the unique varieties of plants and animals make their lifestyles very different from those who inhabit the lowland forest.

THE DIVERSITY OF RAIN FOREST PEOPLE

Early Rain Forest People

No one really knows where the first rain forest people came from, or how they colonized the forests. It is not easy to find the remains of early people because warmth and moisture in the forest have helped break down organic matter, leaving few clues for archeologists to study. Generations of people appear to have lived and died in the rain forests without leaving a mark on their surroundings.

Many scientists think that people moved from the savannah grasslands into the rain forests about one million years ago. However, in the Amazon region, there is only evidence that people have inhabited this region for 15–20,000 years.

▲ Many Amazonian Indians, such as this Kayapo man, wear face paint and elaborate decorations for rituals and ceremonies.

◀ The remains of a complex of pyramids at Palenque in the rain forest of southern Mexico. It was built by the Mayas at the peak of their civilization, over 1,000 years ago.

But people of African origin may have been living here for thousands of years longer than the evidence suggests. It would have been possible for African fishermen to get blown across the Atlantic and survive the journey, or for other great ocean travelers, such as the Polynesians from the Pacific, to have landed and settled in South America.

The First Amazonians

Most scientists, however, believe the first Amazonians migrated from Asia up to 20,000 years ago, crossing the Bering Strait into North America before moving south to populate South and Central America.

RAIN FOREST SECRETS

SECRET SOCIETY

Some traditional rain forest beliefs have existed as long as the rain forest people, and have spread across continents.

Today, in the rain forest villages of Cameroon in West Africa, a cult known as Ekpe, or the Leopard Cult, practices. In this traditional rain forest cult, figures dressed as leopard spirits perform energetic dances at ceremonies.

Variations of this cult were taken to other countries between the 16th and 18th centuries by slaves who were forced to work on the sugar plantations of South and Central America and the Caribbean .

The culture of the people descended from African slaves lives on in the form of beliefs and cults such as voodoo, a famous secret society in the Caribbean that is based on the culture of West Africa.

A rubber tapper in a remote part of the Amazonian rain forest feeding his pigs and poultry. His ancestors moved here from northeast Brazil at the end of the 19th century.

This rain forest family is partly of Indian and partly of European descent.

The Start of Rain Forest Agriculture

The first people who entered the rain forests from the savannah probably lived as hunter-gatherers. Rain forest agriculture is believed to have started in Africa about 2,500 years ago when a tribal group called the Bantu increased in size, and began moving into the edges of the rain forest in search of land for agriculture.

In the Amazon rain forest, agriculture is thought to have developed about 2,000 years ago. However, it is possible that agriculture has been practiced here for much longer than this.

The Europeans Arrive

The lifestyle of rain forest people remained undisturbed for thousands of years. However, in the 15th century, colonists from Europe began to explore the world for new lands and trade. When they first arrived in South America in 1492, there were probably between 12 and 15 million Amazonian Indians living in the Amazon basin. Their numbers were to be devastated by centuries of colonization by European settlers who exploited the resources of the rain forest and its people.

▲ *A young Kaxinawa Indian boy in Brazil.*

Rubber and Slavery

The Amazonian Indians discovered latex—the white sticky fluid from the rubber tree. Later, Europeans realized how useful latex could be in industry, which led to a "rubber boom" in the Amazon. More than half a million people, mainly from the poor northeast of Brazil, headed for the Amazon rain forest in search of work as rubber latex collectors in the late 1800s. Many of these workers, plus tens of thousands of Amazonian Indians, became slaves of the Europeans. Large numbers died, as a result of either cruel treatment or disease. The lives of most of the Amazonian Indians who survived were changed forever. Many of the Europeans intermarried with the Indians, and a new kind of rain forest person—the *caboclo*—was created.

RAIN FOREST SECRETS

CABOCLOS

Caboclos, descendants of indigenous people, and Europeans or Africans, are sometimes called the "forgotten people" of the Brazilian Amazon. Tens of thousands of caboclos live in the Amazon today. Many do not exist "officially" because they do not have identity cards. Nor is their way of life as well known as that of traditional rain forest people. Many make a living in small fishing communities, while others collect rubber or Brazil nuts.

While the newer migrants who enter the rain forest often convert forest into farmland, caboclos have lifestyles that are very similar to those of traditional rain forest people, causing little change or damage to their surroundings.

RAIN FOREST SECRETS

THE MALAGASY PEOPLE

Archeologists believe that the first people to populate the giant island of Madagascar, off the east coast of Africa, arrived about 1,500 years ago. They came from Indonesia and Malaysia in Southeast Asia. Later migrations came from other parts of Asia and East Africa.

The island's inhabitants are called the Malagasy people, and they are very diverse in terms of their origin and appearance. Today, there are 16 distinct ethnic groups on the island. Nine of them live in the rain-forested areas,

which are now rice paddies and look quite similar to the land left behind in Southeast Asia by some of the Malagasy's ancestors.

Changing the Traditions

As European settlers colonized areas of rain forest, they also set up plantations and mines to exploit natural resources like timber and oil. They built places to live, roads, and railways, and introduced new religions such as Christianity. These changes greatly altered the lives of the rain forest people. In South and Central America, not only did Europeans arrive and intermarry with local Indians, they also brought millions of slaves from Africa to work on plantations. In Brazil, for example, an estimated five million slaves were imported between 1542 and 1850, and today many caboclos are of mixed descent.

Fascinating Fact

Within the first ten years of the 21st century, it is estimated that more than one million people will move from overcrowded parts of Indonesia to the island of Irian Jaya.

This family from northeast Brazil settled in the Atlantic rain forest on Bahia's coast.

In the Amazonian city of Belem, a large part of the population, including this girl, are descended from local Indians and either African or European settlers.

20th-Century Settlers

Over the last five hundred years, millions of settlers have moved into the world's rain forests, but the greatest migrations have occurred in the 20th century. The main reason people move into the rain forests today is to escape poverty and overcrowding in towns and cities. Every year, millions of people migrate from the towns in search of forest land, which they clear in order to grow food. Governments of rain forest countries, such as Indonesia and Brazil, have set up programs to encourage people to leave overcrowded areas in this way.

However, there is not always enough land available due to the way it is distributed. Migrants are not allowed to move to the best land, because this is already claimed by powerful landowners. In the state of Bahia in Brazil, there are a quarter of a million people looking for land to move to. Many have no other choice but to move to the Atlantic rain forest on Bahia's coast.

3 THE RAIN FOREST HABITAT

The Variety of the Rain Forest

Rain forest people live in a wide variety of habitats, including the mangrove forests of tropical coastlines, lowland forest in the Amazon basin, and the cooler montane forests found in countries such as Rwanda in Africa and Colombia and Peru in South America. Each is home to people who have adapted to living in their environment.

Traditional rain forest people have had to develop special skills to identify thousands of plants and animals in their habitat. They remember which plants cannot be eaten, when certain types of trees bear fruit, which insects and reptiles are poisonous, and how to hunt rain forest animals successfully.

▲ *In the middle of the rain forest, most settlements are found along the banks of rivers.*

▶ *A view of the interior of dry lowland forest, near the Amazon city of Manaus in Brazil. It is often called* terra firme *forest.*

THE SOLOMON ISLANDERS

In many parts of the Solomon Islands, local people have a lifestyle known as "subsistence affluence." This is when the rain forest and the coastal waters are so plentiful in food that the people do not need to spend many hours a day cultivating, collecting, or hunting food.

The diet of Solomon Islanders consists mainly of fish caught from coral reefs, sweet potatoes cultivated in small rain forest gardens, and coconuts gathered from trees that line the beaches where villages are located.

Dry-Ground Forest

Most Amazonian rain forest is *terra firme,* meaning "dry-ground forest." This forest has heavy rainfall, but rarely floods, and usually has soil that is poor in nutrients. Because of this, rain forest people move regularly so they will not exhaust the land. Terra firme forest tends to have only a few large, wild animals per acre, and rain forest people have learned to hunt them. These animals, such as deer, hide well in undergrowth and can move quickly. Hunting requires great skill and local knowledge in order to locate, kill, and collect food successfully.

LIVING IN THE FLOODED FOREST

People living in the flooded forest have cleverly adapted their lives to suit the seasons. For example, fish can be caught throughout the year. In the dry season, fish are trapped in lakes, while in the wet season, when the rivers flood, they are caught as they migrate to their breeding sites in the upper Amazon river.

Other activities also depend on the seasons. In the dry season, the inhabitants plant and harvest crops in their gardens and graze cattle on the exposed grasslands. In the wet season, cattle are kept on floating rafts while silt from the floodwater provides nutrients for the soils in the gardens. People can stay in their villages because the houses are built on stilts.

Flooded Forest

Some areas of the Amazon rain forest are underwater for several months each year. They are called the flooded forest or *várzea*. Here, the water levels of the rivers and lakes rise and fall between the dry and wet seasons. In the wet season, the floods form a large temporary lake in the upper Amazon.

Tens of thousands of people—indigenous inhabitants, caboclos, and settlers—live in the flooded forest of the Amazon. To survive, they have had to adapt their lives to this remarkable environment. Their houses are typically built on the highest ridges of land, resting on stilts that lift them clear of the water in the flooded season.

Fascinating Fact

Some scientists believe that millions of years ago, the Amazon basin was a vast area of water, dotted with islands.

▲ These men from a village in the flooded forest of the Amazon are making a dugout canoe so they can travel across the region.

▶ (Above right) A woman standing in her garden in front of an area of cloud forest near Pasto in Colombia.

Montane Forest

Montane, or cloud, forests, such as those in Tanzania, Ecuador, and Madagascar, are as rich in trees and plants as lowland forests, but the species are often very different. The undergrowth is much more tangled than in terra firme forests, and this makes traveling around much more difficult. Unlike people in the lowland forest, montane forest inhabitants cannot move by boat on large, meandering rivers. The cooler temperatures also mean that potatoes and hardier plants are often grown instead of manioc (cassava), which is a staple food in lowland forests. In general, life is harder for the people of montane forests, and communities tend to be small and fairly isolated.

4 IN HARMONY WITH THE RAIN FOREST

◀ A man climbs an acai palm tree to harvest the large bundles of fruit, which are sold to make a delicious drink rich in vitamins.

Rain Forest Activities

Rain forest people have many different ways of making a living. Their activities include fishing, hunting, collecting wild foods such as nuts and fruits, and cultivating small gardens cut out of the forest. Rain forest people spend much of their time tending these small forest gardens, which typically contain a large number of useful plants, like manioc, maize, and beans, as well as fruit and palm trees and some medicinal plants. After a few years, new planting is abandoned because the nutrients in the soil are used up. The people move on, leaving their gardens to return to forest. However, people will come back to their forest gardens for many years after they have left to collect fruit from the trees they previously planted.

▼ A typical rain forest garden where a small area of forest is given over to growing manioc.

KAYAPO INDIANS

The Kayapo Indians of the Brazilian Amazon have developed a highly planned system of forest management.

They have gardens near their villages where they grow manioc, tobacco, sweet potatoes, and many other kinds of plants. As various crops mature, they are harvested at different times, from several months to several years after planting. The Kayapo Indians continue to collect fruit from their gardens long after they have left the village to find more fertile soil. They also gather hundreds of wild fruits, nuts, and leaves from the forest, as well as many medicinal plants.

Fascinating Fact

Kayapo villagers from a large village may blaze up to 300 miles (483 km) of trails in order to collect forest plants.

Other Activities

Rain forest people may also grow cash crops such as coffee, cacao, and cotton in their small gardens to sell to traders or as local produce. Some catch fish from the rivers to sell in local markets. These activities can be in harmony with the forest if the areas cultivated are not too large and the use of fertilizers and pesticides is kept to a minimum. Some small-scale farmers and collectors of fruits and nuts work for large international industries—such as rubber and rattan companies.

Collecting Rain Forest Products

Rain forest people collect a huge range of products from the forest. Most are food items or building materials. Foods such as wild fruits, honey, and mushrooms are collected to add variety to people's diets and provide essential vitamins and minerals. Other products, such as vines and palm leaves, are used to make twine, nets, baskets, and sleeping mats. Firewood and medicinal plants are also found in the forest. Many of these products are used by rain forest people themselves or sold to improve their incomes.

In the Amazon rain forest, international industries have grown up around a number of rain forest products. Tens of thousands of people are employed for part of the year gathering Brazil nuts and tapping latex from wild rubber trees. Other industries focus on the valuable palm fruits from the forest.

◀ A rubber tapper holds a ball of rubber he has processed. The latex has been smoked to turn it from liquid into a sticky consistency.

Fascinating Fact

Brazil nut trees do not produce nuts on plantations or in areas where the rain forest has been cut down around them.

▼ Latex being collected in the Amazon rain forest. The rubber tapper scores the bark of the rubber tree and collects the latex, which is a milky sap, in a small cup.

Extractive Reserves

In some parts of the Amazon, the government recognizes certain areas as "extractive reserves." These reserves provide rain forest people with a living, but are used in ways that protect the land in the long term.

Many of these reserves were created following the murder of the rubber tapper Chico Mendes in the Brazilian state of Acre

LINKS

Poison Medicine

Modern medicine uses products from the rain forests. One such product is curare, which is collected from rain forest vines that grow in Peru and Brazil. A colorless liquid called tubocurarine is extracted from the curare and used in surgeries around the world. The way the chemical works is to relax all the muscles in the body with the exception of those that pump the heart. This allows surgeons to carry out delicate operations because the patient's body is completely immobilized.

Amazonian Indians have a different use for curare. They scrape the bark of particular vines, pound it, and then extract the toxic liquid to use as poison in their hunting darts.

in 1988. Chico Mendes was a famous rain forest campaigner who lived near the town of Xapuri. This is where the extractive reserve named after him has been established. Within the reserve, people have the right to collect products that are renewable, such as rubber latex, palm fruit, and Brazil nuts. The extractive reserve also has legal protection from loggers, ranchers, and soy farmers who continue to destroy other parts of the forest.

Local fishermen in the flooded forest of the upper Amazon catch certain types of fish using a bow and arrow.

An Amazonian fisherman holding a tambaqui fish, which he caught using a harpoon.

Rain Forest Fishing

Fishing is one of the main activities of rain forest people. The Amazon basin has more than 300,000 miles (500,000 km) of waterways, with thousands of small fishing communities dotted along them.

More than 4,000 species of fish live in the rivers of the Amazon rain forest, including the giant pirarucu and many different types of piranha. In order to catch the different varieties of fish, rain forest people use spears, bows and arrows, poisons, and harpoons. Nets and fish traps made from local materials are also used.

Mangrove forests are particularly rich in fish species. The forests are used as breeding and nursery sites for fish that are important for people's livelihoods. Small, traditional fishing communities are well aware of the value of mangrove forests, and they fish in a way that allows the forest to survive and the fish to breed successfully.

FRUIT-EATING FISH

Every year in Brazil, the rivers near Manaus rise. The Amazon and its tributaries form a huge seasonal lake. When the forest is flooded, more than 2,000 types of fish swim through the underwater trees. Some fish have adapted to eating the fruit and nuts that fall in the water. The people in the fishing community of Aracampinas, near Santarem, have decided to plant hundreds of fruit trees, not for people but for fish.

A community spokeswoman said, "Fish numbers have been declining because of deforestation and overfishing. . . . Our community has decided to replant the wild fruit trees and to protect breeding lakes, so that there will be sufficient fish when our children grow up."

Fascinating Fact

Fishermen in the flooded forest of the Amazon use a simple harpoon to catch giant pirarucu fish. These fish can be over 10 feet (3 m) in length and weigh 330 pounds (150 kg).

Hunting

Rain forest hunters have to be extremely skillful. The number of large prey in any area of rain forest is usually very low, and many animals hide high up in the canopy. Traditional rain forest people use a number of weapons for hunting, including bows and arrows, blowpipes, spears, and traps. Most hunters have strict rules about when certain animals can be hunted, and limit the number that can be caught. This helps keep the population of important animals at a sustainable level, and allows hunters to continue with their lifestyle in the future.

23

Housing

The homes of rain forest people vary from small, moveable hunting huts made from a framework of branches covered with leaves, to huge structures over 130 feet (40 m) long that can house entire villages. The Mehinaku Indians in Brazil and the Dyaks in Borneo have traditionally lived in large communal houses. But many rain forest people, such as the Penan of Sarawak, are semi-nomadic and use natural materials to build simple shelters. These break down naturally after they have been abandoned, and new shelters are built. In this way, the impact of the homes and villages of traditional people on the rain forest is kept to a minimum. However, the materials used to build rain forest homes can depend on what is locally available. In West Africa, people live in homes with clay walls, which form more permanent dwellings.

▲ A Yanomami village in Brazil. The main house in a Yanomami Indian village is called a Yano. It is the largest house and can hold more than 100 people.

▼ The settlers in this remote part of the Amazon rain forest used local materials to build their home.

Transportation

Rain forest people often travel over long distances. To do this, they walk along simple forest trails or travel by river in various types of boats. In central areas of many lowland rain forests, people often use dugout canoes. Along the coasts, many people have developed ocean-going sailing boats, such as the dhows used off the mangrove-lined coasts of East Africa. These traditional modes of transportation are made from local forest materials and do not produce any pollution.

▲ *The rivers are the highways of the lowland forests. Most families have boats to transport them around the forest.*

RAIN FOREST SECRETS

WAR CANOE OF THE MAORIS

One of the largest dugout canoes ever built is a Maori war canoe (or waka) called *Ngatokimstawhaoura*, named after one of the rain forest spirits. It can still be seen at Waitangi, New Zealand. Measuring over 100 feet (30.5 m) long, it is made from three separate trunks of rain forest Kauri trees. It is so large that it can hold eighty warriors.

In 1820, Major Richard Cruise, from onboard his ship, the H.M.S. *Dromedary*, described the sight of a Maori war canoe in action: "The largest we saw was 84 feet (26 m) long . . . made from a single Kauri tree . . . propelled by ninety men . . . . The canoe moved with astonishing rapidity, causing the water to foam on either side of it." The canoe is still an impressive sight, when it is put in the water every year as part of Maori celebrations.

Sustaining the Rain Forest

There are many ways of using the rain forest in a sustainable way. For example, it is possible to use timber from a rain forest without destroying the whole forest. Unfortunately, loggers have already deforested huge areas of land. Today, some timber companies realize that if they do not conserve natural forests there will only be plantation forests in the future. Some people buy timber only from areas of well-managed forest, which now exist all over the world. In southern Mexico, many community-run forests are producing commercial timber and chicle (for chewing gum) in ways that protect the environment. In the Amazon, several logging companies have adopted a new system in which only a few valuable trees per acre are removed, leaving the rest of the forest undisturbed.

▲ An area in the Amazon where commercial timber has been removed without destroying the rest of the forest.

▼ Each log from a well-managed forest is labeled, and the number of trees cut from any area is strictly controlled.

RAIN FOREST SECRETS

THE PEOPLE OF NOVEK

In the 1950s, many farmers in Mexico were attracted to the timber industry in the south of the country. They took jobs working for a big logging company, cutting down many trees and earning a small wage. In 1982, the villagers became the owners of the forest and started to manage it themselves as a community. Their area of rain forest, called Novek, has now gradually regenerated.

The people of Novek are receiving a much better income for carrying out the same type of work they did for the logging company. They work in a way that cares for the environment, cutting down fewer trees each year than before. By cleverly managing the land, they can earn an income while protecting the forest.

Ecotourism

Many tourists will pay to visit spectacular rain forests and their traditional people. In Panama, the Kuna Indians of the San Blas Islands allow tourists to visit parts of their land. The Kuna own the legal rights to their traditional lands and can control the number of visitors.

For ecotourism to work, the interests of the local people and the environment need to be respected. Unfortunately, in Brazil the Amazonian Indians do not own any land themselves and can be exploited by tour operators.

▼ *These visitors are enjoying the rain forest scenery. Ecotourism in rain forests around the world creates local employment and does not destroy the forest.*

EXPLOITING RAIN FOREST PEOPLE

◄ *Some rain forest people today have access to satellite television. This kind of influence is altering their view of the world and, in some areas, undermining their culture.*

Endangered Lifestyles

The traditional lifestyles of many rain forest people have been changed by the activities of the powerful people who manage the forests. Today, many rain forests have roads running through them. They are plundered for resources such as minerals, timber, and oil. Dams and pipelines are being built, and rivers are being polluted with toxic materials. All these activities make the livelihoods of traditional rain forest people very uncertain.

Disappearing Forests and People

For people who live in the rain forests or who collect rain forest products for a living, deforestation means losing their way of life and their means of survival. Where possible, rain forest people move deeper into the forest in order to keep their culture and lifestyle. However, most of them have no choice but to work for large landowners or in timber sawmills for poor pay. Many end up living in the slums of rain forest cities.

▼ *Deforestation in the Amazon is forcing indigenous people to migrate out of the forest.*

▲ *Waorani Indians in the South American country of Ecuador have had their culture affected by the arrival of missionaries in the rain forest.*

Another problem that threatens the survival of rain forest people is the introduction of diseases against which they have no resistance. "Western" diseases have devastated communities for centuries, and even today many rain forest people have no immunity against illnesses such as flu, tuberculosis, and measles.

There are other unwelcome influences. Rain forest people believe in respecting the forest, living in harmony with nature, and using the plants and animals sparingly. Influences such as "western style" education and beliefs often undermine traditional culture and values.

RAIN FOREST SECRETS

THE WEYEWA AND RITUAL SPEAKING

Lindi Mbartu is an elder of the Weyewa indigenous people, who live in a fragment of rain forest on the island of Sumba in Indonesia. The Weyewa have an ancient tradition of ritual speaking, which passes on aspects of their culture to younger generations in the form of stories told in their own language. Today, however, this oral history is threatened because young Weyewa people are taught in the national language of Indonesia. This is seen as a way of uniting a country that has more than 13,000 islands and hundreds of languages. But it means that part of the Weyewa culture and tradition is in danger of dying out.

Rain Forest Destruction

Governments of rain forest countries often allow companies to cut timber and mine precious resources on a large scale. Sometimes they do this to help pay back money borrowed from the world's wealthiest countries. In some countries, such as Brazil, the government regards cutting down the Amazon rain forest as part of becoming a developed nation. People from outside the rain forest earn vast amounts of money by removing its timber and minerals. However, it is unusual for local people to benefit from these activities for more than a few years.

The main causes of rain forest destruction include converting the forest to agricultural land, ranching, logging, fires, and mining. The building of roads, dams, pipelines, and urban settlements also cause great damage. Rain forest people are often used as cheap labor or are presented as "curiosities" for tourists.

▲ The timber industry is one of the main causes of deforestation and has caused serious problems for rain forest people and their way of life. ▼

SHIPIBO TOURIST VILLAGES

In Peru, tourists who visit the Amazonian town of Pucallpa are offered a chance to see "real" Amazonian Indians. Tours are arranged to Shipibo Indian villages to see people making beautiful clay pots decorated in the distinct geometrical designs of the Shipibo.

However, the Shipibo have lost most of their rain forest lands to loggers, colonists, and ranchers, and their culture has been changed by outsiders. They now have little choice but to let themselves be offered as tourist attractions. Many people think the Amazonian Indians should have the right to own the land they inhabit and to live on it as they wish, without having to provide a spectacle for tourists.

▼ New settlers cut down large areas of forest in order to grow food. The land they cultivate is often not suitable for their crops.

Logging

Logging is one of the most obvious causes of rain forest destruction. In countries such as the Philippines, Thailand, Venezuela, Australia, and Cameroon, huge areas of forest have been destroyed by loggers. Unfortunately, logging techniques are often very crude, which means whole areas are felled just to extract a few trees that can be sold. Rain forest timber is in great demand in Europe, North America, Japan, and increasingly, in China. The timber is used as raw material in products such as paper, cellulose, and plywood. This demand has led to massive destruction of the tropical rain forests.

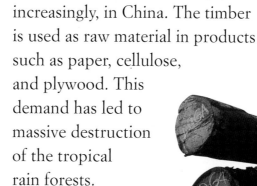

Large populations are changing many areas of African and Asian rain forests into agriculture land.

Many homeless people, such as this man in the Brazilian state of Bahia, cut down forest to grow food for their starving families.

From Rain Forest to Agricultural Land

Throughout the world, large areas of rain forest are being changed into agricultural land. However, the soil is generally too poor to support crops for more than a few years. In some parts of the world, each person may be cutting down over an acre (.5 hectare) of rain forest every year to support crops or make forest gardens.

In West Africa, the increasing number of people who live in, or have recently moved into, the rain forest are causing serious deforestation. This is threatening the lifestyles of people in long-established villages. Because there is only a limited supply of forest and an increasing number of inhabitants, there is a risk that the forest will be completely replaced by agricultural land. Often, the new arrivals do not have the same expertise as traditional people in managing natural resources for the future. Many areas of African rain forest, as elsewhere, are cleared to make way for large plantations of commercial crops such as pineapples and bananas.

LINKS

Oil Palm Plantations

Many forests have been cut down to make way for oil palm plantations. The African oil palm thrives in places where rainfall is high. Commercial plantations (see right) have been developed in countries such as Cameroon, Ecuador, Malaysia, and Indonesia. Oil comes from both the flesh and the kernel of the oil palm (see far right). It is now one of the main sources of vegetable oil and can also be used in products such as cookies, soap, margarine, and shampoo.

The African oil palm is well suited to rain forest conditions, because it can survive in poor soil. But after only a few years the soil needs to be treated with fertilizers. In many areas, it is cheaper to cut down a new area of forest and create a new plantation than it is to pay for the fertilizer.

This has been a major cause of deforestation in Malaysia and Indonesia in recent years.

Powerful Landowners and Landless People

In the Amazon rain forest, powerful landowners are rapidly clearing the forest for new soy bean farms. They are also forcing many Brazilian families to move away from good agricultural land so that they can make their estates bigger.

In Brazil, 4.5 percent of the landowners own 81 percent of all farmland. However, most rural families own no land at all. Landless people are forced to cut down areas of rain forest in an effort to feed their families.

◀ A ranch hand rounds up
cattle in an area that was once
Amazonian rain forest.

Cowboys and Cattle

Ranching is one of the greatest threats to the rain forest and
its people in Central and South America. Cattle need huge
areas of land to graze in, and they consume large amounts
of grain and soy from big plantations. Tens of thousands of
acres of forest in Central America have been burned down
to make way for cattle ranches. Much of the beef from
countries such as Costa Rica and Panama is exported for
use in fast-food hamburgers and in pet foods.

In the Amazon, ranching is a disaster for the rain forest,
destroying people's homes and livelihoods. Furthermore,
the number of people who are employed per acre on the
ranches is only a fraction of the number that could be
supported by collecting nuts, fruits, and rubber in a
standing rain forest.

Fascinating Fact

There are 100,000
cattle ranches in
Amazonia. Each animal
requires at least
12 acres (five hectares)
of land to survive.

LINKS

Chocolate and the Forest

Chocolate is made from the seeds that grow in the pods of the cacao tree (see below right). The cultivation of cacao has helped to preserve the rain forest and provide employment for tens of thousands of people in the tropics. This is because the cacao plants need to grow in the shade of rain forest trees. However, in 1997 cacao plants growing in the Atlantic rain forest in Brazil became infected with a virus that quickly destroyed them. Thousands of people lost their jobs, and much of the forest was destroyed to make way for ranching or crops such as bananas (see above right) that do not need the shade of rain forest trees.

▼ A fish market near Santarem, Brazil. When the Amazon floods, the fish feed on fruit and forest litter. If the forest is cleared, the fish do not get the food they need to survive and fish stocks suffer.

Fish and Wild Animals

Wild resources are often overexploited. For example, large fishing fleets in the Amazon catch tons of fish each year with little thought for managing fish stocks for the future. In African cities, the trade in rain forest "bush meat," such as deer, monkeys, and even manatees (aquatic animals), is reducing food for traditional hunters and causing damage to the environment. The poaching of rare animals, such as tigers for their skins and bears for their organs, is another threat to the rain forests and their people.

The discovery of oil in the rain forest of Ecuador has led to the pollution of rivers and the growth of towns like Lago Agrio.

Large-scale gold mining in the rain forest of Pocone, Brazil is causing hardship to many local Indians and other rain forest people.

Big Plans

Many politicians and large businesses look at the rain forest only in terms of money. They think an untapped rain forest is a waste of resources. International businesses and organizations often think the same way, and have loaned large amounts of money to some countries to build roads, dams for hydroelectric power, pipelines, and mines in order to develop the economy.

Many of these gigantic projects were badly planned. For example, when the Tucurui dam in Brazil was built, the developers did not think about the trees in the valley that would be flooded. Nearly 3 million square yards (2.5 million cubic meters) of prime timber was left underwater. The tannin from the trees made the lake highly acidic, which, in turn, corroded the generating turbines of the Tucurui dam.

LINKS

The Road to Extinction

Road building has had a particularly serious effect on Amazonian Indians. A new road between the cities of Manaus and Caracarai, for example, was built straight through the territory of the Wairmiri Atroari Indians. In just a few years, their numbers were reduced from over 3,000 to less than 350 people.

In 2001, the Brazilian government announced a huge road building program for the Amazon region, as part of "Advance Brazil." This will cause great

problems to many other Amazonian Indians, such as the Yanomami and Kaxinawa.

Making the Problem Worse

Road building almost always encourages settlers to move into new parts of the rain forest. It speeds up the loss of the forest, and leads to increased burning along the edges of roads to control plant growth. More settlers help pollute the rivers and spread fatal diseases to rain forest people. Roads also mean the lifestyles of traditional people are disturbed or destroyed. In the case of the Yanomami Indians in Brazil, new roads allowed thousands of gold miners to move onto their land, destroying the forest, polluting the rivers with mercury, and even killing Yanomami people themselves. Many of their groups now have so few people that the Yanomami may disappear completely from large parts of the Brazilian Amazon region that was once their home.

Fascinating Fact

During the wet season, many of Brazil's roads become flooded and have to be closed to traffic. Some roads are even washed away.

CONSERVATION OF THE RAIN FOREST

The community of Aracampinas, near Santarem in Brazil, has built an environmental center to teach children about the plants and animals that live in the rain forest.

In the town of Xapuri, local people have organized a Brazil nut-processing factory, run as a cooperative, so that the whole community can enjoy the economic benefits.

The Situation Today

At the beginning of the 21st century, the situation for many traditional and other rain forest people is very serious. However, many local inhabitants are taking action to improve their lives while retaining their culture. Where rain forest people have gained legal rights to their land they can choose how they want to live. They may combine their traditional lives with some of the advantages of the modern world, if they wish. This can include having medical centers, that offer western medicine to deal with illnesses such as measles or flu, alongside their own time-tested remedies.

In addition to local activities, there are many individuals and international organizations that are campaigning on behalf of rain forest people. They are putting pressure on governments, large companies, and powerful landowners to recognize rain forest people's basic human and land rights.

Cooperative Action

A number of rain forest people have formed cooperatives to sell their products. For example, the Kayapo Indians sell Brazil nuts to Fair Trade organizations. Rubber tappers in Brazil have also formed cooperatives to help conserve their way of life. Cooperatives allow groups of rain forest people to keep some aspects of their lifestyle while earning money to help the community as a whole. Some groups, such as the Kaxinawa, live deep in the Brazilian forest but sell their goods made from wild rubber via the Internet.

RAIN FOREST SECRETS

WOMEN'S GROUPS ON MAFIA ISLAND

The mangrove island of Mafia lies off the coast of Tanzania in the Indian Ocean. Here, some villages have formed women's groups that make mats and baskets, which they sell to tourists visiting the island. They also fish for octopus to help pay for the materials they need. The money they have earned has helped build a storehouse, a meeting room, and a better medical center.

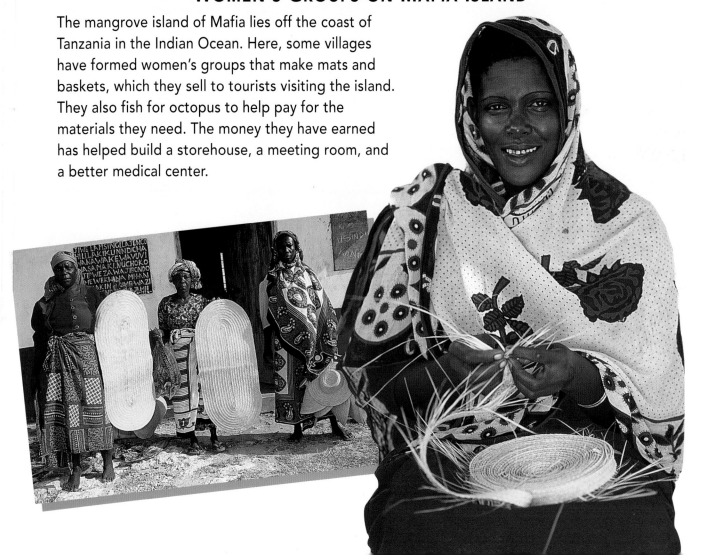

Land Rights

Of all the actions that need to be taken, the most important is to recognize the rights of rain forest people to their traditional lands. This is what they continually ask for. It is only by knowing they cannot be forced off their lands that rain forest people have any chance to fight against the pressures of the outside world. They can choose how they use their own rain forest resources and what aspects of the outside world, if any, they would like to adopt.

Education

The role of education for rain forest people is very important. But in many countries, the kind of education that rain forest children receive is not well suited to their lifestyle. This is because it suggests that traditional activities are not really valuable.

 A village near Andapa in Madagascar, where the community has gained the land rights and is now managing its own rain forest.

The World Wildlife Fund (WWF) has provided environmental education training for many schoolteachers who work with rain forest communities, such as this one at Seringal in northern Brazil.

A FISHING VILLAGE IN MEXICO

In Celestun, a fishing village on the mangrove coast of southeast Mexico, the children learn about the environment in the small primary school. The village revolves around fishing for octopus, crabs, and a variety of commercial fish. It is important for the children to learn how to manage the fish stocks and protect the mangrove forest, because fishing and tourism will be their future if they stay in the village. Some students will work in the fish-packing plant but many others will fish and work as guides for the tourists who come to see the town's spectacular lagoon.

Some people suggest that it is not modern and efficient to collect rain forest products in a traditional way. Such views have led many rain forest people to leave their lands, mistakenly believing that life in a town or city may be better. However, other programs recognize that children should be able to feel proud of their culture and way of life. They are also taught about the benefits and problems associated with a "western" style of life. In this way, rain forest people have the chance to choose their lifestyle and decide whether to live in a traditional way or to make a change. Organizations such as the World Wildlife Fund (WWF) and Oxfam help fund rain forest environmental education programs in remote areas.

◀ Internationally famous, the Chico Mendes Extractive Reserve near Xapuri in Brazil provides a model for other rain forest communities to follow. It is protected from development, but allows renewable resources to be collected.

Campaigning Organizations

There are many organizations that try to help rain forest people survive and keep their traditional way of life. Survival International, Oxfam, and Christian Aid are just some of the groups campaigning to protect rain forest homes and help the people gain recognition of their land rights.

Several organizations, including major religious, human rights, and environmental groups, are calling for debt repayments to be cancelled for the poorest countries of the world. This would help slow down the destruction of the rain forest, which occurs when countries try to pay back large debts by selling their forest resources. The WWF has also successfully petitioned governments of many rain forest countries to provide "gifts of land" to traditional rain forest people.

Fascinating Fact

A letter-writing campaign organized by Survival International resulted in the government of Colombia granting the Nukac people a large area of rain forest.

▼ International environmental organizations are supporting communities involved in sustainable use of their forests, such as collecting Brazil nuts.

INHERITOR CHILDREN FROM COLOMBIA

High in the cloud forests of southern Colombia, a group of children are making an impact on local society. Around a lake called La Cocha, about one hundred children have organized themselves into a group called "The Inheritors of the Planet." Supported by the WWF, they have campaigned to protect their cloud forest from the practice of making charcoal, which is destructive to the forest. They also work on environmental projects, such as replanting trees. They meet and talk to other children about how to protect their rain forest, and in this way guard their long-term future.

What Can You Do?

You can help rain forest people by supporting some of the organizations that campaign on their behalf. Another way is to buy products such as Fair Trade coffee and "certified" timber. The producers of these goods all recognize the land and community rights of rain forest people and are working to help them achieve their goals.

⑦ THE FUTURE

Uncertain Future

Rain forests are important to everyone in the world, whether we live in them or not. The World Conservation Monitoring Center estimates that nearly one million acres (400,000 hectares) of rain forest in the Amazon is cut down every year. This makes the future of the inhabitants very uncertain. Although they face many problems, rain forest people are trying to find ways to solve them. In many places they have formed organizations to ensure that their rights to the land and way of life are recognized, so they can plan a future for themselves. As part of this process, rain forest people have offered important ideas about how the forest can be safeguarded, and how some of the damage that has been done to their forests and traditions can be repaired.

◀ One of the young people belonging to the group called "The Inheritors of the Planet" in Colombia.

▼ Collecting vines used for brushes and baskets. The future of rain forests such as the Amazon depends on everybody using their resources sustainably.

RAIN FOREST SECRETS

THE UDZUNGWA MOUNTAIN NATIONAL PARK IN TANZANIA

Along the edge of the Udzungwa Mountain National Park, children are learning how to protect their environment and way of life. The park authorities let the children enter the park to carry out many traditional activities such as collecting mushrooms and fruit.

For two days a week, people are allowed to collect fallen branches and dead wood for firewood. Children at the school are planting trees along the edge of the park near their villages so they will have access to firewood and timber when they grow up.

Amazon Initiatives

In the Amazon, Indians and other rain forest people, such as rubber tappers, have been working together to protect the forest and their lifestyles. In Brazil, a number of campaigning organizations such as the "Forest People's Alliance" have been formed. This organization calls for rain forest people to take part in government decisions. It also believes that colonizers of the forest should be taught how to live there without destroying it. The organization recommends that large projects such as dams be cancelled, and that the remaining forest be protected for the future.

GLOSSARY

A cultural event by the Weyera in Indonesia.

archeologists People who study human history by looking for remains of ancient human activity.

bush meat A term for meat from wild animals, which are killed for human consumption.

caboclo A Brazilian word for the descendants of a marriage between an Amazonian Indian and a settler.

campaigner A person who tries to raise public and political awareness about a cause or an issue.

canopy The layer of trees between the forest floor and the tallest towering treetops.

cash crops Products such as cotton and sugar, which are sold as a way of earning income.

certified Wood that comes from an area of forest that is officially recognized as being well managed.

chicle The sticky sap from a rain forest tree, which is the raw material used to make chewing gum.

colonize To move into an area and set up a new community.

commercial crops Crops such as coffee and soya, which have a high value when sold on the market.

cooperative A business owned and run by a group of people, who share the profits between them.

ecotourism When tourists visit natural environments with an interest in conserving them.

extinct When the species of any living organism, such as an animal, a tree, or a plant no longer exists.

fertilizers Substances added to the soil to make it more fertile for growing crops.

indigenous Belonging originally or naturally to a particular place.

mangrove A swamp forest found on tropical and subtropical tidal mud flats.

nomadic A lifestyle of roaming from place to place, often looking for new pastures or agricultural land.

nursery sites Areas where young animals or fish grow up in relative security.

nutrients Any substances that provide essential nourishment for living organisms.

organic A crop or method of animal production that does not involve the use of artificial chemicals.

plantations Farms or estates where crops are cultivated.

poachers People who illegally hunt or collect animals, fish, or plants.

rain forest garden A small garden that is cultivated in a rain forest area.

ranching Farming that is primarily involved in cattle breeding and rearing for meat.

rattan The tough, flexible stem of a climbing palm, collected mainly for making furniture.

savannah Open grassland in tropical or subtropical areas where few trees or bushes grow.

slaves People who are the legal property of others and forced to work for no money.

slums Poor urban areas of housing, where people often live without good access to basic services.

species A group of animals or plants that closely resemble one another.

sustainable A way of using resources that does not threaten their long term availability, or the survival of the plants, animals, or people who depend on them.

voodoo A type of religious witchcraft practiced by the descendants of slaves in the Caribbean.

FURTHER INFORMATION

BOOKS TO READ

Chinery, Michael. *People and Places: Secrets of the Rainforest.* New York: Crabtree Publishers, 2000.

George, Jean Craighead. *One Day in the Tropical Rainforest.* New York: HarperCollins Publishers, 1995.

Greenaway, Theresa. *Jungle.* New York: Dorling Kindersley Publishing, 2000.

Knight, Tim. *Journey into the Rainforest.* New York: Oxford University Press, 2001.

Lewington, Anna. *Antonio's Rainforest.* Minneapolis, MN: Lerner Publishing Group, 1996.

Lewington, Anna. *People of the Rainforests.* New York: Raintree Steck-Vaughn, 1998.

Morrison, Marion. *The Amazon Rainforest: And Its People.* New York: Raintree Steck-Vaughn, 1993.

Sauvain, Phillip. *Geography Detective: Rain Forests.* Minneapolis, MN: Carolrhoda Books, Inc., 1997.

Wood, Selina. *The Rainforest.* Brookfield, CT: Millbrook Press, 1997.

VIDEO

National Geographic's Amazon: Land of the Flooded Forest. National Geographic Video, 1990.

ORGANIZATIONS

Friends of the Earth
1025 Vermont Avenue, N.W., Suite 300
Washington, D.C. 20005-6303
Tel: 202-783-7400
www.foe.org

Greenpeace
702 H Street, N.W.
Washington, D.C. 20001
Tel: 1-800-326-0959
www.greenpeaceusa.org/

Oxfam America
1112 16th Street, N.W.
Suite 600
Washington, D.C. 20036
Tel: 202-496-1180
www.oxfamamerica.org

World Wildlife Fund
1250 24th Street, N.W.
Washington, D.C. 20037
Tel: 202-293-4800
www.worldwildlife.org

INDEX